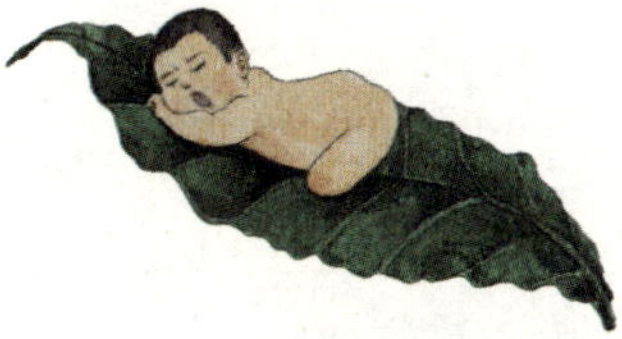

新月集

文／【印】泰戈尔　译／郑振铎　图／史　怡

中国青年出版社

（京）新登字 083 号

图书在版编目（CIP）数据

新月集：汉、英 /（印）泰戈尔著；郑振铎译著．—
北京：中国青年出版社，2021.7
ISBN 978-7-5153-6448-3

Ⅰ．①新…　Ⅱ．①泰…②郑…　Ⅲ．①英语－汉语－
对照读物②诗集－印度－现代　Ⅳ．① H319.4：Ⅰ

中国版本图书馆 CIP 数据核字（2021）第 147949 号

责任编辑　侯群雄　张睿智
封面设计　史　怡

出版发行　中国青年出版社
社　　址　北京东四十二条 21 号　邮政编码：100708
网　　址　www.cyp.com.cn
门 市 部　010-57350370
编 辑 部　010-57350401
印　　刷　三河市君旺印务有限公司
经　　销　新华书店
规　　格　660 × 970　1/16
印　　张　10
字　　数　100 千字
版　　次　2021 年 9 月北京第 1 版
印　　次　2021 年 9 月河北第 1 次印刷
定　　价　28.00 元

译序一

我对于泰戈尔诗最初发生浓厚的兴趣，是在第一次读《新月集》的时候。那时离现在将近五年；许地山君坐在我家的客厅里，长发垂到两肩，在黄昏的微光中对我谈到泰戈尔的事。他说，他在缅甸时，看到泰戈尔的画像，又听人讲到他，便买了他的诗集来读。过了几天，我到许地山君的宿舍里去。他说："我拿一本泰戈尔的诗选送给你。"他便到书架上去找那本诗集。我立在窗前，四围静悄悄的，只有水池中喷泉的潺潺的声音。我很寂静的[①]在等候读那美丽的书。他不久便从书架上取下很小的一本绿纸面的书来，他说："这是一个日本人选的泰戈尔诗，你先拿去看看。泰戈尔不多几时前曾到过日本。"我坐了车回家，在归途中，借着新月与市灯的微光，约略的把它翻看了一遍。最使我喜欢的是它当中所选的几首《新月集》的诗。那一夜，在灯下又看了一次。第二天，地山见我时，问道："你最喜欢那[②]几首？"我说："《新月集》的几首。"他隔了几天，又拿了一本很美丽的书给我，他说："这就是《新月集》。"从那时后，《新月集》便常在我的书桌上；直到现在，我还时时把它翻开来读。

① 的，旧时可表"地（de）"之义。（本书注释均为编者注。）

② 那，旧时同"哪"。

我译《新月集》也是受地山君的鼓励。有一天，他把他所译的《吉檀迦利》的几首诗给我看，都是用古文译的。我说："译得很好，但似乎太古奥了。"他说："这一类的诗，应该用古奥的文体译。至于《新月集》，却又须用新妍流露的文字译。我想译《吉檀迦利》，你为何不译《新月集》呢？"于是我与他约，我们同时动手译这两部书。此后二年中，他的《吉檀迦利》固未译成，我的《新月集》，也时译时辍。直至《小说月报》改革后，我才把自己所译的《新月集》在它上面发表了几首。地山译的《吉檀迦利》却始终没有再译下去，已译的几首，也始终不肯拿出来发表。许多朋友却时时的催我把这个工作做完。那时我正有选译泰戈尔诗的计划，便一方面把旧译稿整理一下，一方面又新译了八九首出来；结果便成了现在的这个译本。

我喜欢《新月集》，如我之喜欢安徒生的童话。安徒生的文字美丽而富有诗趣。他有一种不可测的魔力，能把我们带到美丽和平的花的世界、虫的世界、人鱼的世界里去；能使我们随了他走进有静的方池的绿水、有美的挂在黄昏的天空的雨后弧虹等等的天国里去。《新月集》也具有这种不可测的魔力。它把我们从怀疑、贪婪的罪恶的世界，带到秀嫩天真的儿童的新月之国里去。它能使我们重复回到坐在泥土里以枯枝断梗为戏的时代；它能使我们在心里重温着在海滨以贝壳为餐具，以落叶为舟，以绿草上的露点为圆珠的儿童的梦。总之，我们只要一翻开它来，便立刻如得到两只有魔术的翼膀，可以使自己飞翔到美静天真的儿童国里去。而这个儿童的天国便是作者的一个理想国。

我应该向许地山君表示谢意；他除了鼓励我以外，在这个译本写好时，还曾为我校读了一次。

一九二三年八月二十二日

译序二

我在一九二三年的时候，曾把泰戈尔的《新月集》译为中文出版。但在那个译本里，并没有把这部诗集完全译出。这部诗集的英文本共有诗四十首，我只译出了三十一首。现在把我的译本重行校读了一下，重译并改正了不少地方，同时，并把没有译出的九首也补译了出来。这可算是《新月集》的一部比较完整的译本了。

应该在这里谢谢孙家晋同志，他花了好几天的工夫，把我的译文仔细的校读了一遍，有好几个地方是采用了他的译法的。

一九五四年八月六日

目录

家 庭

我独自在横跨过田地的路上走着，夕阳像一个守财奴似的，正藏起它的最后的金子。

白昼更加深沉的没入黑暗之中，那已经收割了的孤寂的田地，默默的躺在那里。

天空里突然升起了一个男孩子的尖锐的歌声。他穿过看不见的黑暗，留下他的歌声的辙痕跨过黄昏的静谧。

他的乡村的家坐落在荒凉的土地的边上，在甘蔗田的后面，躲藏在香蕉树、瘦长的槟榔树、椰子树和深绿色的贾克果[①]树的阴影里。

我在星光下独自走着的路上停留了一会，我看见黑沉沉的大地展开在我的面前，用她的手臂拥抱着无量数的家庭，在那些家庭里有着摇篮和床铺，母亲们的心和夜晚的灯，还有年轻轻的生命，他们满心欢乐，却浑然不知这样的欢乐对于世界的价值。

---

① 贾克果，即波罗蜜。

THE HOME

I paced alone on the road across the field while the sunset was hiding its last gold like a miser.

The daylight sank deeper and deeper into the darkness, and the widowed land, whose harvest had been reaped, lay silent.

Suddenly a boy's shrill voice rose into the sky. He traversed the dark unseen, leaving the track of his song across the hush of the evening.

His village home lay there at the end of the waste land, beyond the sugar-cane field, hidden among the shadows of the banana and the slender areca palm, the cocoa-nut and the dark green jack-fruit trees.

I stopped for a moment in my lonely way under the starlight, and saw spread before me the darkened earth surrounding with her arms countless homes furnished with cradles and beds, mothers' hearts and evening lamps, and young lives glad with a gladness that knows nothing of its value for the world.

海 边

孩子们会集在无边无际的世界的海边。

无垠的天穹静止的临于头上，不息的海水在足下汹涌。孩子们会集在无边无际的世界的海边，叫着，跳着。

他们拿沙来建筑房屋，拿空贝壳来做游戏。他们把落叶编成了船，笑嘻嘻的把它们放到大海上。孩子们在世界的海边，做他们的游戏。

他们不知道怎样泅水，他们不知道怎样撒网。采珠的人为了珠潜水，商人在他们的船上航行，孩子们却只把小圆石聚了又散。他们不搜求宝藏；他们不知道怎样撒网。

大海哗笑着涌起波浪，而海滩的微笑荡漾着淡淡的光芒。致人死命的波涛，对着孩子们唱无意义的歌曲，就像一个母亲在摇动她孩子的摇篮时一样。大海和孩子们一同游戏，而海滩的微笑荡漾着淡淡的光芒。

孩子们会集在无边无际的世界的海边。狂风暴雨飘游在无辙迹的天空上，航船沉碎在无辙迹的海水里，死正在外面活动，孩子们却在游戏。在无边无际的世界的海边，孩子们大会集着。

ON THE SEASHORE

On the seashore of endless worlds children meet.

The infinite sky is motionless overhead and the restless water is boisterous. On the seashore of endless worlds the children meet with shouts and dances.

They build their houses with sand, and they play with empty shells. With withered leaves they weave their boats and smilingly float them on the vast deep. Children have their play on the seashore of worlds.

They know not how to swim, they know not how to cast nets. Pearl-fishers dive for pearls, merchants sail in their ships, while children gather pebbles and scatter them again. They seek not for hidden treasures, they know not how to cast nets.

The sea surges up with laughter, and pale gleams the smile of the sea-beach. Death-dealing waves sing meaningless ballads to the children, even like a mother while rocking her baby's cradle.

The sea plays with children, and pale gleams the smile of the sea-beach.

On the seashore of endless worlds children meet. Tempest roams in the pathless sky, ships are wrecked in the trackless water, death is abroad and children play. On the seashore of endless worlds is the great meeting of children.

来 源

流泛在孩子两眼的睡眠，——有谁知道它是从什么地方来的？是的，有个谣传，说它是住在萤火虫朦胧的照耀着林荫的仙村里，在那个地方，挂着两个迷人的懊怯的蓓蕾。它便是从那个地方来吻孩子的两眼的。

当孩子睡时，在他唇上浮动着的微笑——有谁知道它是从什么地方生出来的？是的，有个谣传，说新月的一线年青的清光，触着将消未消的秋云边上，于是微笑便初生在一个浴在清露里的早晨的梦中了。——当孩子睡时，微笑便在他的唇上浮动着。

甜蜜柔嫩的新鲜生气，像花一般的在孩子的四肢上开放着——有谁知道它在什么地方藏得这样久？是的，当妈妈还是一个少女的时候，它已在爱的温柔而沉静的神秘中，潜伏在她的心里了。——甜蜜柔嫩的新鲜生气，像花一般的在孩子的四肢上开放着。

THE SOURCE

The sleep that flits on baby's eyes—does anybody know from where it comes? Yes, there is a rumour that it has its dwelling where, in the fairy village among shadows of the forest dimly lit with glow-worms, there hang two shy buds of enchantment. From there it comes to kiss baby's eyes.

The smile that flickers on baby's lips when he sleeps—does anybody know where it was born? Yes, there is a rumour that a young pale beam of a crescent moon touched the edge of a vanishing autumn cloud, and there the smile was first born in the dream of a dew-washed morning—the smile that flickers on baby's lips when he sleeps.

The sweet, soft freshness that blooms on baby's limbs—does anybody know where it was hidden so long? Yes, when the mother was a young girl it lay pervading her heart in tender and silent mystery of love—the sweet, soft freshness that has bloomed on baby's limbs.

孩童之道

只要孩子愿意，他此刻便可飞上天去。

他所以不离开我们，并不是没有原故。

他爱把他的头倚在妈妈的胸间，他即使是一刻不见她，也是不行的。

孩子知道各式各样的聪明话，虽然世间的人很少懂得这些话的意义。

他所以永不想说，并不是没有原故。

他所要做的一件事，就是要学习从妈妈的嘴唇里说出来的话。那就是他所以看来这样天真的原故。

孩子有成堆的黄金与珠子，但他到这个世界上来，却像一个乞丐。

他所以这样假装了来，并不是没有原故。

这个可爱的小小的裸着身体的乞丐，所以假装着完全无助的样子，便是想要乞求妈妈的爱的财富。

孩子在纤小的新月的世界里，是一切束缚都没有的。

他所以放弃了他的自由，并不是没有原故。

他知道有无穷的快乐藏在妈妈的心的小小一隅里，被妈妈亲爱的手臂所拥抱，其甜美远胜过自由。

孩子永不知道如何哭泣。他所住的是完全的乐土。

他所以要流泪，并不是没有原故。

虽然他用了可爱的脸儿上的微笑，引逗得他妈妈的热切的心向着他，然而他的因为细故而发的小小的哭声，却编成了怜与爱的双重约束的带子。

BABY'S WAY

If baby only wanted to, he could fly up to heaven this moment.

It is not for nothing that he does not leave us.

He loves to rest his head on mother's bosom, and cannot ever bear to lose sight of her.

Baby knows all manner of wise words, though few on earth can understand their meaning.

It is not for nothing that he never wants to speak.

The one thing he wants is to learn mother's words from mother's lips. That is why he looks so innocent.

Baby had a heap of gold and pearls, yet he came like a beggar on to this earth.

It is not for nothing he came in such a disguise.

This dear little naked mendicant pretends to be utterly helpless, so that he may beg for mother's wealth of love.

Baby was so free from every tie in the land of the tiny crescent moon.

It was not for nothing he gave up his freedom.

He knows that there is room for endless joy in mother's little corner of a heart, and it is sweeter far than liberty to be caught and pressed in her dear arms.

Baby never knew how to cry. He dwelt in the land of perfect bliss.

It is not for nothing he has chosen to shed tears.

Though with the smile of his dear face he draws mother's yearning heart to him, yet his little cries over tiny troubles weave the double bond of pity and love.

不被注意的花饰

啊，谁给那件小外衫染上颜色的，我的孩子，谁使你的温软的肢体穿上那件红的小外衫的？

你在早晨就跑出来到天井里玩儿，你，跑着就像摇摇欲跌似的。

但是谁给那件小外衫染上颜色的，我的孩子？

什么事叫你大笑起来的，我的小小的命芽儿？

妈妈站在门边，微笑的望着你。

她拍着她的双手，她的手镯叮当的响着，你手里拿着你的竹竿儿在跳舞，活像一个小小的牧童儿。

但是什么事叫你大笑起来的，我的小小的命芽儿？

喔，乞丐，你双手攀搂住妈妈的头颈，要乞讨些什么？

喔，贪得无厌的心，要我把整个世界从天上摘下来，像摘一个果子似的，把它放在你的一双小小的玫瑰色的手掌上么？

喔，乞丐，你要乞讨些什么？

风高兴的带走了你踝铃的叮当。

太阳微笑着，望着你的打扮。

当你睡在你妈妈的臂湾里时，天空在上面望着你，而早晨蹑手蹑脚的走到你的床跟前，吻着你的双眼。

风高兴的带走了你踝铃的叮当。

仙乡里的梦婆飞过朦胧的天空，向你飞来。

在你妈妈的心头上，那世界母亲，正和你坐在一块儿。

他，向星星奏乐的人，正拿着他的横笛，站在你的窗边。

仙乡里的梦婆飞过朦胧的天空，向你飞来。

THE UNHEEDED PAGEANT

Ah, who was it coloured that little frock, my child, and covered your sweet limbs with that little red tunic?

You have come out in the morning to play in the courtyard, tottering and tumbling as you run.

But who was it coloured that little frock, my child?

What is it makes you laugh, my little life-bud?

Mother smiles at you standing on the threshold.

She claps her hands and her bracelets jingle, and you dance with your bamboo stick in your hand like a tiny little shepherd.

But what is it makes you laugh, my little life-bud?

O beggar, what do you beg for, clinging to your mother's neck with both your hands?

O greedy heart, shall I pluck the world like a fruit from the sky to place it on your little rosy palm?

O beggar, what are you begging for?

The wind carries away in glee the tinkling of your anklet bells.

The sun smiles and watches your toilet.

The sky watches over you when you sleep in your mother's arms, and the morning comes tiptoe to your bed and kisses your eyes.

The wind carries away in glee the tinkling of your anklet bells.

The fairy mistress of dreams is coming towards you, flying through the twilight sky.

The world-mother keeps her seat by you in your mother's heart.

He who plays his music to the stars is standing at your window with his flute.

And the fairy mistress of dreams is coming towards you, flying through the twilight sky.

偷睡眠者

谁从孩子的眼里把睡眠偷了去呢？我一定要知道。

妈妈把她的水罐挟在腰间，走到近村汲水去了。

这是正午的时候。孩子们游戏的时间已经过去了；池中的鸭子沉默无声。

牧童躺在榕树的荫下睡着了。

白鹤庄重而安静的立在檬果[①]树边的泥泽里。

就在这个时候，偷睡眠者跑来从孩子的两眼里捉住睡眠，便飞去了。

当妈妈回来时，她看见孩子四肢着地的在屋里爬着。

谁从孩子的眼里把睡眠偷了去呢？我一定要知道。我一定要找到她，把她锁起来。

我一定要向那个黑洞里张望，在这个洞里，有一道小泉从圆的和有皱纹的石上滴下来。

我一定要到醉花[②]林中的沉寂的树影里搜寻，在这林中，鸽

① 檬果，即杧果。

② 醉花，即香榄的花。在印度传说中，当香榄被洒以年轻女子口中的甘酒，其花始盛开。

子在它们住的地方咕咕的叫着，仙女的脚环在繁星满天的静夜里叮当的响着。

我要在黄昏时，向静静的萧萧的竹林里窥望，在这林中，萤火虫闪闪的耗费它们的光明，只要遇见一个人，我便要问他，“谁能告诉我偷睡眠者住在什么地方？”

谁从孩子的眼里把睡眠偷了去呢？我一定要知道。

只要我能捉住她，怕不会给她一顿好教训！

我要闯入她的巢穴，看她把所有偷来的睡眠藏在什么地方。

我要把它都夺来，带回家去。

我要把她的双翼缚得紧紧的，把她放在河边，然后叫她拿一根芦苇在灯心草和睡莲间钓鱼为戏。

黄昏，街上已经收了市，村里的孩子们都坐在妈妈的膝上时，夜鸟便会讥笑的在她耳边说：

“你现在还想偷谁的睡眠呢？”

SLEEP-STEALER

Who stole sleep from baby's eyes? I must know.

Clasping her pitcher to her waist, mother went to fetch water from the village near by.

It was noon. The children's playtime was over; the ducks in the pond were silent.

The shepherd boy lay asleep under the shadow of the *banyan* tree.

The crane stood grave and still in the swamp near the mango grove.

In the meanwhile the Sleep-stealer came and, snatching sleep from baby's eyes, flew away.

When mother came back she found baby travelling the room over on all fours.

Who stole sleep from our baby's eyes? I must know. I must find her and chain her up.

I must look into that dark cave, where, through boulders and scowling stones, trickles a tiny stream.

I must search in the drowsy shade of the *bakula* grove, where pigeons coo in their corner, and fairies' anklets tinkle in the stillness of starry nights.

In the evening I will peep into the whispering silence of the bamboo forest, where fireflies squander their light, and will ask every creature I meet, "Can anybody tell me where the Sleep-stealer lives?"

Who stole sleep from baby's eyes? I must know.

Shouldn't I give her a good lesson if I could only catch her!

I would raid her nest and see where she hoards all her stolen sleep.

I would plunder it all, and carry it home.

I would bind her two wings securely, set her on the bank of the river, and then let her play at fishing with a reed among the rushes and water-lilies.

When the marketing is over in the evening, and the village children sit in their mothers' laps, then the night birds will mockingly din her ears with:

"Whose sleep will you steal now?"

开 始

“我是从那儿来的，你，在那儿把我检[1]起来的？”孩子问他的妈妈说。

她把孩子紧紧的搂在胸前，半哭半笑的答道——

“你曾被我当作心愿藏在我的心里，我的宝贝。

“你曾存在于我孩童时代玩的泥娃娃身上；每天早晨我用泥土塑造我的神像，那时我反覆的塑了又捏碎了的就是你。

“你曾和我们的家庭守护神一同受到祀奉，我崇拜家神时也就崇拜了你。

“你曾活在我所有的希望和爱情里，活在我的生命里，我母亲的生命里。

“在主宰着我们家庭的不死的精灵的膝上，你已经被抚育了好多代了。

“当我做女孩子的时候，我的心的花瓣儿张开，你就像一股花香似的散发出来。

“你的软软的温柔，在我青春的肢体上开花了，像太阳出来之前的天空上的一片曙光。

---

① 检，旧时同“捡”。

“上天的第一宠儿，晨曦的孪生兄弟，你浮泛世界的生命的溪流而下，终于停泊在我的心头。

“当我凝视你的脸蛋儿的时候，神秘之感湮没了我；你这属于一切人的，竟成了我的。

“为了怕失掉你，我把你紧紧的搂在胸前。是什么魔术把这世界的宝贝引到我这双纤小的手臂里来呢？”

THE BEGINNING

"Where have I come from, where did you pick me up?" the baby asked its mother.

She answered half crying, half laughing, and clasping the baby to her breast,—

"You were hidden in my heart as its desire, my darling.

You were in the dolls of my childhood's games; and when with clay I made the image of my god every morning, I made and unmade you then.

You were enshrined with our household deity, in his worship I worshipped you.

In all my hopes and my loves, in my life, in the life of my mother you have lived.

In the lap of the deathless Spirit who rules our home you have been nursed for ages.

When in girlhood my heart was opening its petals, you hovered as a fragrance about it.

Your tender softness bloomed in my youthful limbs, like a glow in the sky before the sunrise.

Heaven's first darling, twin-born with the morning light, you have floated down the stream of the world's life, and at last you have stranded on my heart.

As I gaze on your face, mystery overwhelms me; you who belong to all have become mine.

For fear of losing you I hold you tight to my breast. What magic has snared the world's treasure in these slender arms of mine?"

孩子的世界

我愿我能在我孩子自己的世界的中心，占一角清净地。

我知道有星星同他说话，天空也在他面前垂下，用它傻傻的云朵和彩虹来娱悦他。

那些大家以为他是哑的人，那些看去像是永不会走动的人，都带了他们的故事，捧了满装着五颜六色的玩具的盘子，匍匐的来到他的窗前。

我愿我能在横过孩子心中的道路上游行，解脱了一切的束缚；

在那儿，使者奉了无所谓的使命奔走于无史的诸王的王国间；

在那儿，理智以她的法律造为纸鸢而飞放，真理也使事实从桎梏中自由了。

BABY'S WORLD

I wish I could take a quiet corner in the heart of my baby's very own world.

I know it has stars that talk to him, and a sky that stoops down to his face to amuse him with its silly clouds and rainbows.

Those who make believe to be dumb, and look as if they never could move, come creeping to his window with their stories and with trays crowded with bright toys.

I wish I could travel by the road that crosses baby's mind, and out beyond all bounds;

Where messengers run errands for no cause between the kingdoms of kings of no history;

Where Reason makes kites of her laws and flies them, and Truth sets Fact free from its fetters.

时候与原因

当我给你五颜六色的玩具的时候，我的孩子，我明白了为什么云上水上是这样的色彩缤纷，为什么花朵上染上绚烂的颜色的原因了——当我给你五颜六色的玩具的时候，我的孩子。

当我唱着使你跳舞的时候，我真的知道了为什么树叶儿响着音乐，为什么波浪把它们的合唱的声音送进静听着的大地的心头的原因了——当我唱着使你跳舞的时候。

当我把糖果送到你贪得无厌的双手上的时候，我知道了为什么在花萼里会有蜜，为什么水果里会秘密的充溢了甜汁的原因了——当我把糖果送到你贪得无厌的双手上的时候。

当我吻着你的脸蛋儿叫你微笑的时候，我的宝贝，我的确明白了在晨光里从天上流下来的是什么样的快乐，而夏天的微飔吹拂在我的身体上的又是什么样的爽快——当我吻着你的脸蛋儿叫你微笑的时候。

WHEN AND WHY

When I bring you coloured toys, my child, I understand why there is such a play of colours on clouds, on water, and why flowers are painted in tints—when I give coloured toys to you, my child.

When I sing to make you dance, I truly know why there is music in leaves, and why waves send their chorus of voices to the heart of the listening earth—when I sing to make you dance.

When I bring sweet things to your greedy hands, I know why there is honey in the cup of the flower, and why fruits are secretly filled with sweet juice—when I bring sweet things to your greedy hands.

When I kiss your face to make you smile, my darling, I surely understand what pleasure streams from the sky in morning light, and what delight the summer breeze brings to my body—when I kiss you to make you smile.

责 备

为什么你眼里有了眼泪，我的孩子？

他们真是可怕，常常无谓的责备你！

你写字时墨水玷污了你的手和脸——这就是他们所以骂你龌龊的原故么？

呵，呸！他们也敢因为圆圆的月儿用墨水涂了脸，便骂她龌龊么？

他们总要为了每一件小事去责备你，我的孩子。他们总是无谓的寻人错处。

你游戏时扯破了你的衣服——这就是他们所以说你不整洁的原故么？

呵，呸！秋之晨从他的破碎的云衣中露出微笑，那末，他们要叫他什么呢？

他们对你说什么话，尽管可以不去理睬他，我的孩子。

他们把你做错的事长长的记了一笔账。

谁都知道你是十分喜欢糖果的——这就是他们所以称你做贪婪的原故么？

呵，呸！我们是喜欢你的，那末，他们要叫我们什么呢？

DEFAMATION

Why are those tears in your eyes, my child?

How horrid of them to be always scolding you for nothing!

You have stained your fingers and face with ink while writing—is that why they call you dirty?

O, fie! Would they dare to call the full moon dirty because it has smudged its face with ink?

For every little trifle they blame you, my child. They are ready to find fault for nothing.

You tore your clothes while playing—is that why they call you untidy?

O, fie! What would they call an autumn morning that smiles through its ragged clouds?

Take no heed of what they say to you, my child.

They make a long list of your misdeeds.

Everybody knows how you love sweet things—is that why they call you greedy?

O, fie! What then would they call us who love you?

审判官

你想说他什么尽管说罢[1]，但是我知道我孩子的短处。

我爱他并不因为他好，只是因为他是我的小小的孩子。

你如果把他的好处与坏处两两相权一下，恐怕你就会知道他是如何的可爱罢?

当我必须责罚他的时候，他更成为我的生命的一部分了。

当我使他眼泪流出时，我的心也和他同哭了。

只有我才有权去骂他，去责罚他，因为只有热爱人的才可以惩戒人。

① 罢，旧时同“吧（ba）”。

THE JUDGE

Say of him what you please, but I know my child's failings.

I do not love him because he is good, but because he is my little child.

How should you know how dear he can be when you try to weigh his merits against his faults?

When I must punish him he becomes all the more a part of my being.

When I cause his tears to come my heart weeps with him.

I alone have a right to blame and punish, for he only may chastise who loves.

玩 具

孩子，你真是快活呀，一早晨坐在泥土里，耍着折下来的小树枝儿。

我微笑的看你在那里耍着那根折下来的小树枝儿。

我正忙着算账，一小时一小时在那里加叠数字。

也许你在看我，想道："这种好没趣的游戏，竟把你的一早晨的好时间浪费掉了！"

孩子，我忘了聚精会神玩耍树枝与泥饼的方法了。

我寻求贵重的玩具，收集金块与银块。

你呢，无论找到什么便去做你的快乐的游戏，我呢，却把我的时间与力气都浪费在那些我永不能得到的东西上。

我在我的脆薄的独木船里挣扎着要航过欲望之海，竟忘了我也是在那里做游戏了。

PLAYTHINGS

Child, how happy you are sitting in the dust, playing with a broken twig all the morning.

I smile at your play with that little bit of a broken twig.

I am busy with my accounts, adding up figures by the hour.

Perhaps you glance at me and think, "What a stupid game to spoil your morning with!"

Child, I have forgotten the art of being absorbed in sticks and mud-pies.

I seek out costly playthings, and gather lumps of gold and silver.

With whatever you find you create your glad games, I spend both my time and my strength over things I never can obtain.

In my frail canoe I struggle to cross the sea of desire, and forget that I too am playing a game.

天文家

我不过说："当傍晚圆圆的满月挂在劫丹波[①]的枝头时，有人能去捉住它么？"

哥哥却对我笑道："孩子呀，你真是我所见到的顶顶傻的孩子。月亮离我们这样远，谁能去捉住它呢？"

我说："哥哥，你真傻！当妈妈向窗外探望，微笑着往下看我们游戏时，你也能说她远么？"

哥哥还是说："你这个傻孩子！但是，孩子，你到那里去找一个大得能逮住月亮的网呢？"

我说："你自然可以用双手去捉住它呀。"

但是哥哥还是笑着说："你真是我所见到的顶顶傻的孩子！如果月亮走近了，你便知道它是多末大了。"

我说："哥哥，你们学校里所教的，真是没有用呀！当妈妈低下脸儿跟我们亲嘴时，她的脸看来也是很大的么？"

但是哥哥还是说："你真是一个傻孩子。"

① 劫丹波，即团花树，是印度教神话中的圣树。

THE ASTRONOMER

I only said, "When in the evening the round full moon gets entangled among the branches of that *Kadam* tree, couldn't somebody catch it?"

But dādā laughed at me and said, "Baby, you are the silliest child I have ever known. The moon is ever so far from us, how could anybody catch it?"

I said, "Dādā, how foolish you are! When mother looks out of her window and smiles down at us playing, would you call her far away?"

Still dādā said, "You are a stupid child! But, baby, where could you find a net big enough to catch the moon with?"

I said, "Surely you could catch it with your hands."

But dādā laughed and said, "You are the silliest child I have known. If it came nearer, you would see how big the moon is."

I said, "Dādā, what nonsense they teach at your school! When mother bends her face down to kiss us does her face look very big?"

But still dādā says, "You are a stupid child."

云与波

妈妈，住在云端的人对我唤道——

“我们从醒的时候游戏到白日终止。

“我们与黄金色的曙光游戏，我们与银白色的月亮游戏。”

我问道：“但是，我怎么能够上你那里去呢？”

他们答道：“你到地球的边上来，举手向天，就可以被接到云端里来了。”

“我妈妈在家里等我呢，”我说，“我怎么能离开她而来呢？”

于是他们微笑着浮游而去。

但是我知道一件比这个更好的游戏，妈妈。

我做云，你做月亮。

我用两只手遮盖你，我们的屋顶就是青碧的天空。

住在波浪上的人对我唤道——

“我们从早晨唱歌到晚上；我们前进前进的旅行，也不知我们所经过的是什么地方。”

我问道：“但是，我怎么能加入你们队伍里去呢？”

他们告诉我说：“来到岸旁，站在那里，紧闭你的两眼，你就被带到波浪上来了。”

我说：“傍晚的时候，我妈妈常要我在家里——我怎么能离开她而去呢？”

于是他们微笑着，跳舞着奔流过去。

但是我知道一件比这个更好的游戏。

我是波浪，你是陌生的岸。

我奔流而进，进，进，笑哈哈的撞碎在你的膝上。

世界上就没有一个人会知道我们俩在什么地方。

CLOUDS AND WAVES

Mother, the folk who live up in the clouds call out to me—

"We play from the time we wake till the day ends.

We play with the golden dawn, we play with the silver moon."

I ask, "But, how am I to get up to you?"

They answer, "Come to the edge of the earth, lift up your hands to the sky, and you will be taken up into the clouds."

"My mother is waiting for me at home," I say. "How can I leave her and come?"

Then they smile and float away.

But I know a nicer game than that, mother.

I shall be the cloud and you the moon.

I shall cover you with both my hands, and our house-top will be the blue sky.

The folk who live in the waves call out to me—

"We sing from morning till night; on and on we travel and know not where we pass."

I ask, "But, how am I to join you?"

They tell me, "Come to the edge of the shore and stand with your eyes tight shut, and you will be carried out upon the waves."

I say, "My mother always wants me at home in the evening—how can I leave her and go?"

Then they smile, dance and pass by.

But I know a better game than that.

I will be the waves and you will be a strange shore.

I shall roll on and on and on, and break upon your lap with laughter.

And no one in the world will know where we both are.

金色花

假如我变了一朵金色花[1]，只是为了好玩，长在那棵树的高枝上，笑哈哈的在风中摇摆，又在新生的树叶上跳舞，妈妈，你会认识我么？

你要是叫道：“孩子，你在那里呀？”我暗暗的在那里匿笑，却一声儿不响。

我要悄悄的开放花瓣儿，看着你工作。

当你沐浴后，湿发披在两肩，穿过金色花的林荫，走到你做祷告的小庭院时，你会嗅到这花的香气，却不知道这香气是从我身上来的。

当你吃过中饭，坐在窗前读《罗摩衍那》[2]，那棵树的阴影落在你的头发与膝上时，我便要投我的小小的影子在你的书页上，正投在你所读的地方。

但是你会猜得出这就是你的小孩子的小影子么？

当你黄昏时拿了灯到牛棚里去，我便要突然的再落到地上来，又成了你的孩子，求你讲个故事给我听。

---

① 金色花，即黄兰，在印度可用于敬奉神明。

② 《罗摩衍那》，与《摩诃婆罗多》并列为两大印度史诗，主要叙述王子罗摩与其妻子悉多的故事。

“你到那里去了，你这坏孩子？”

“我不告诉你，妈妈。”这就是你同我那时所要说的话了。

THE CHAMPA FLOWER

Supposing I became a *champa* flower, just for fun, and grew on a branch high up that tree, and shook in the wind with laughter and danced upon the newly budded leaves, would you know me, mother?

You would call, "Baby, where are you?" and I should laugh to myself and keep quite quiet.

I should slyly open my petals and watch you at your work.

When after your bath, with wet hair spread on your shoulders, you walked through the shadow of the *champa* tree to the little court where you say your prayers, you would notice the scent of the flower, but not know that it came from me.

When after the midday meal you sat at the window reading *Ramayana*, and the tree's shadow fell over your hair and your lap, I should fling my wee little shadow on to the page of your book, just where you were reading.

But would you guess that it was the tiny shadow of your little child?

When in the evening you went to the cowshed with the

lighted lamp in your hand, I should suddenly drop on to the earth again and be your own baby once more, and beg you to tell me a story.

"Where have you been, you naughty child?"

"I won't tell you, mother." That's what you and I would say then.

仙人世界

如果人们知道了我的国王的宫殿在那里，它就会消失在空气中的。

墙壁是白色的银，屋顶是耀眼的黄金。

皇后住在有七个庭院的宫苑里；她戴的一串珠宝，值得整整七个王国的全部财富。

不过，让我悄悄的告诉你，妈妈，我的国王的宫殿究竟在那里。

它就在我们阳台的角上，在那栽着杜尔茜[①]花的花盆放着的地方。

公主躺在远远的隔着七个不可逾越的重洋的那一岸沉睡着。

除了我自己，世界上便没有人能够找到她。

她臂上有镯子，她耳上挂着珍珠；她的头发拖到地板上。

当我用我的魔杖点触她的时候，她就会醒过来，而当她微笑时，珠玉将会从她唇边落下来。

不过，让我在你的耳朵边悄悄的告诉你，妈妈；她就住在我们阳台的角上，在那栽着杜尔茜花的花盆放着的地方。

---

① 杜尔茜，即圣罗勒，印度常见的一种药草，在印度教中被奉为神圣。

当你要到河里洗澡的时候，你走上屋顶的那座阳台来罢。

我就坐在墙的阴影所聚会的一个角落里。

我只让小猫儿跟我在一起，因为它知道那故事里的理发匠住的地方。

不过，让我在你的耳朵边悄悄的告诉你，那故事里的理发匠到底住在那里。

他住的地方，就在阳台的角上，在那栽着杜尔茜花的花盆放着的地方。

FAIRYLAND

If people came to know where my king's palace is, it would vanish into the air.

The walls are of white silver and the roof of shining gold.

The queen lives in a palace with seven courtyards, and she wears a jewel that cost all the wealth of seven kingdoms.

But let me tell you, mother, in a whisper, where my king's palace is.

It is at the corner of our terrace where the pot of the *tulsi* plant stands.

The princess lies sleeping on the far-away shore of the seven impassable seas.

There is none in the world who can find her but myself.

She has bracelets on her arms and pearl drops in her ears; her hair sweeps down upon the floor.

She will wake when I touch her with my magic wand, and jewels will fall from her lips when she smiles.

But let me whisper in your ear, mother; she is there in the

corner of our terrace where the pot of the *tulsi* plant stands.

When it is time for you to go to the river for your bath, step up to that terrace on the roof.

I sit in the corner where the shadows of the walls meet together.

Only puss is allowed to come with me, for she knows where the barber in the story lives.

But let me whisper, mother, in your ear where the barber in the story lives.

It is at the corner of the terrace where the pot of the *tulsi* plant stands.

流放的地方

妈妈，天空上的光成了灰色了；我不知道是什么时候了。

我玩得怪没劲儿的，所以到你这里来了。这是星期六，是我们的休息日。

放下你的活计，妈妈；坐在靠窗的一边，告诉我童话里的特潘塔沙漠在什么地方？

雨的影子遮掩了整个白天。

凶猛的电光用它的爪子抓着天空。

当乌云在轰轰的响着，天打着雷的时候，我总爱心里带着恐惧爬伏到你的身上。

当大雨倾泻在竹叶子上好几个钟头，而我们的窗户为狂风震得格格发响的时候，我就爱独自和你坐在屋里，妈妈，听你讲童话里的特潘塔沙漠的故事。

它在那里，妈妈，在那一个海洋的岸上，在那些个山峰的脚下，在那一个国王的国土里？

田地上没有此疆彼壤的界石，也没有村人在黄昏时走回家的，或妇人在树林里检拾枯枝而捆载到市场上去的道路。沙地

上只有一小块一小块的黄色草地，只有一株树，就是那一对聪明的老鸟儿在那里做窝的，那个地方就是特潘塔沙漠。

我能够想像得到，就在这样一个乌云密布的日子，国王的年轻的儿子，怎样的独自骑着一匹灰色马，走过这个沙漠，去寻找那被囚禁在不可知的重洋之外的巨人宫里的公主。

当雨雾在遥远的天空下降，电光像一阵突然发作的痛楚的痉挛似的闪射的时候，他可记得他的不幸的母亲，为国王所弃，正在扫除牛棚，眼里流着眼泪，当他骑马走过童话里的特潘塔沙漠的时候？

看，妈妈，一天还没有完，天色就差不多黑了，那边村庄的路上没有什么旅客了。

牧童早就从牧场上回家了，人们都已从田地里回来，坐在他们草屋的檐下的草席上，眼望着阴沉的云块。

妈妈，我把我所有的书本都放在书架上了——不要叫我现在做功课。

当我长大了，大得像爸爸一样的时候，我将会学到必须学到的东西的。

但是，今天你可得告诉我，妈妈，童话里的特潘塔沙漠在什么地方？

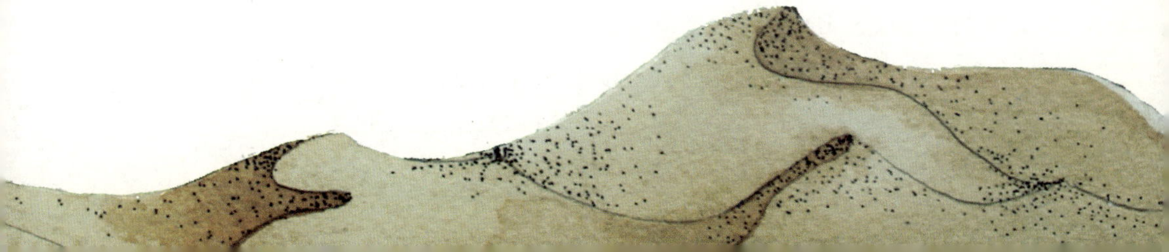

THE LAND OF THE EXILE

Mother, the light has grown grey in the sky; I do not know what the time is.

There is no fun in my play, so I have come to you. It is Saturday, our holiday.

Leave off your work, mother; sit here by the window and tell me where the desert of Tepāntar in the fairy tale is?

The shadow of the rains has covered the day from end to end.

The fierce lightning is scratching the sky with its nails.

When the clouds rumble and it thunders, I love to be afraid in my heart and cling to you.

When the heavy rain patters for hours on the bamboo leaves, and our windows shake and rattle at the gusts of wind, I like to sit alone in the room, mother, with you, and hear you talk about the desert of Tepāntar in the fairy tale.

Where is it, mother, on the shore of what sea, at the foot of what hills, in the kingdom of what king?

There are no hedges there to mark the fields, no footpath across it by which the villagers reach their village in the evening, or the woman who gathers dry sticks in the forest can bring her load to the market. With patches of yellow grass in the sand and only one tree where the pair of wise old birds have their nest, lies the desert of Tepāntar.

I can imagine how, on just such a cloudy day, the young son of the king is riding alone on a grey horse through the desert, in search of the princess who lies imprisoned in the giant's palace across that unknown water.

When the haze of the rain comes down in the distant sky, and lightning starts up like a sudden fit of pain, does he remember his unhappy mother, abandoned by the king, sweeping the cow-stall and wiping her eyes, while he rides through the desert of Tepāntar in the fairy tale?

See, mother, it is almost dark before the day is over, and there are no travellers yonder on the village road.

The shepherd boy has gone home early from the pasture, and men have left their fields to sit on mats under the eaves of their huts, watching the scowling clouds.

Mother, I have left all my books on the shelf—do not ask me to do my lessons now.

When I grow up and am big like my father, I shall learn all that must be learnt.

But just for to-day, tell me, mother, where the desert of Tepāntar in the fairy tale is?

雨 天

乌云很快的集拢在森林的黝黑的边缘上。

孩子，不要出去呀！

湖边的一行棕树，向暝暗的天空撞着头；羽毛零乱的乌鸦，静悄悄的栖在罗望子的枝上，河的东岸正被乌沉沉的暝色所侵袭。

我们的牛系在篱上，高声鸣叫。

孩子，在这里等着，等我先把牛牵进牛棚里去。

许多人都挤在池水泛溢的田间，捉那从泛溢的池中逃出来的鱼儿；雨水成了小河，流过狭衖[①]，好像一个嬉笑的孩子从他妈妈那里跑开，故意要恼她一样。

听呀，有人在浅滩上喊船夫呢。

孩子，天色暝暗了，渡头的摆渡船已经停了。

天空好像是在滂沱的雨上快跑着；河里的水喧叫而且暴躁；妇人们早已拿着汲满了水的水罐，从恒河畔匆匆的回家了。

夜里用的灯，一定要预备好。

---

① 衖（xiàng），同“巷”。

孩子，不要出去呀！

到市场去的大道已没有人走，到河边去的小路又很滑。风在竹林里咆哮着，挣扎着，好像一只落在网中的野兽。

THE RAINY DAY

Sullen clouds are gathering fast over the black fringe of the forest.

O child, do not go out!

The palm trees in a row by the lake are smiting their heads against the dismal sky; the crows with their draggled wings are silent on the tamarind branches, and the eastern bank of the river is haunted by a deepening gloom.

Our cow is lowing loud, tied at the fence.

O child, wait here till I bring her into the stall.

Men have crowded into the flooded field to catch the fishes as they escape from the overflowing ponds; the rain water is running in rills through the narrow lanes like a laughing boy who has run away from his mother to tease her.

Listen, someone is shouting for the boatman at the ford.

O child, the daylight is dim, and the crossing at the ferry is closed.

The sky seems to ride fast upon the madly-rushing rain; the water in the river is loud and impatient; women have hastened home early from the Ganges with their filled pitchers.

The evening lamps must be made ready.

O child, do not go out!

The road to the market is desolate, the lane to the river is slippery. The wind is roaring and struggling among the bamboo branches like a wild beast tangled in a net.

纸 船

我每天把纸船一个个放在急流的溪中。

我用大黑字写我的名字和我住的村名在纸船上。

我希望住在异地的人会得到这纸船，知道我是谁。

我把园中长的秀利花[①]载在我的小船上，希望这些黎明开的花能在夜里平平安安的带到岸上。

我投我的纸船到水里，仰望天空，看见小朵的云正张着满鼓着风的白帆。

我不知道天上有我的什么游伴把这些船放下来同我的船比赛！

夜来了，我的脸埋在手臂里，梦见我的纸船在子夜的星光下缓缓的浮泛前去。

睡仙坐在船里，带着满载着梦的篮子。

① 秀利花，即夜花，通常在夜间开放，天明即脱落。

PAPER BOATS

Day by day I float my paper boats one by one down the running stream.

In big black letters I write my name on them and the name of the village where I live.

I hope that someone in some strange land will find them and know who I am.

I load my little boats with *shiuli* flowers from our garden, and hope that these blooms of the dawn will be carried safely to land in the night.

I launch my paper boats and look up into the sky and see the little clouds setting their white bulging sails.

I know not what playmate of mine in the sky sends them down the air to race with my boats!

When night comes I bury my face in my arms and dream that my paper boats float on and on under the midnight stars.

The fairies of sleep are sailing in them, and the lading is their baskets full of dreams.

水 手

船夫曼特胡的船只停泊在拉琪根琪码头。

这只船无用的装载着黄麻，无所事事的停泊在那里已经好久了。

只要他肯把他的船借给我，我就给它安装一百只桨，扬起五个或六个或七个布帆来。

我决不把它驾驶到愚蠢的市场上去。

我将航行遍仙人世界里的七个大海和十三条河道。

但是，妈妈，你不要躲在角落里为我哭泣。

我不会像罗摩犍陀罗[①]似的，到森林中去，一去十四年才回来。

我将成为故事中的王子，把我的船装满了我所喜欢的东西。

我将带我的朋友阿细和我作伴。我们要快快乐乐的航行于仙人世界里的七个大海和十三条河道。

我将在绝早的晨光里张帆航行。

中午，你正在池塘里洗澡的时候，我们将在一个陌生的国王

① 罗摩犍陀罗，即《罗摩衍那》中的英雄罗摩，传说是印度教主神毗湿奴的第七个化身。

的国土上了。

我们将经过特浦尼浅滩，把特潘塔沙漠抛落在我们的后边。

当我们回来的时候，天色快黑了，我将告诉你我们所见到的一切。

我将越过仙人世界里的七个大海和十三条河道。

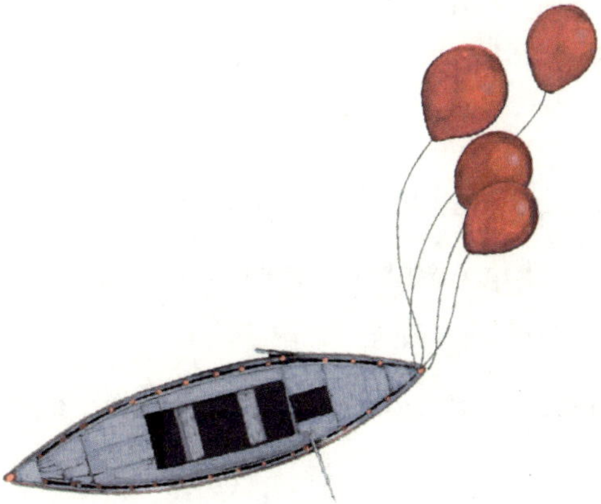

THE SAILOR

The boat of the boatman Madhu is moored at the wharf of Rajgunj.

It is uselessly laden with jute, and has been lying there idle for ever so long.

If he would only lend me his boat, I should man her with a hundred oars, and hoist sails, five or six or seven.

I should never steer her to stupid markets.

I should sail the seven seas and the thirteen rivers of fairyland.

But, mother, you won't weep for me in a corner.

I am not going into the forest like Ramachandra to come back only after fourteen years.

I shall become the prince of the story, and fill my boat with whatever I like.

I shall take my friend Ashu with me. We shall sail merrily across the seven seas and the thirteen rivers of fairyland.

We shall set sail in the early morning light.

When at noontide you are bathing at the pond, we shall be in the land of a strange king.

We shall pass the ford of Tirpurni, and leave behind us the desert of Tepāntar.

When we come back it will be getting dark, and I shall tell you of all that we have seen.

I shall cross the seven seas and the thirteen rivers of fairyland.

对 岸

我渴想到河的对岸去，

在那边，好些船只一行儿系在竹杆上；

人们在早晨乘船渡过那边去，肩上扛着犁头，去耕耘他们的远处的田；

在那边，牧人使他们鸣叫着的牛游泳到河旁的牧场去；

黄昏的时候，他们都回家了，只留下豺狼在这满长着野草的岛上哀叫。

妈妈，如果你不在意，我长大的时候，要做这渡船的船夫。

据说有好些古怪的池塘藏在这个高岸之后，

雨过去了，一群一群的野鹜飞到那里去，茂盛的芦苇在岸边四围生长，水鸟在那里生蛋；

竹鸡带着跳舞的尾巴，将它们细小的足印印在洁净的软泥上；

黄昏的时候，长草顶着白花，邀月光在长草的波浪上浮游。

妈妈，如果你不在意，我长大的时候，要做这渡船的船夫。

我要自此岸至彼岸，渡过来，渡过去，所有村中正在那儿沐浴的男孩女孩，都要诧异的望着我。

太阳升到中天，早晨变为正午了，我将跑到你那里去，说道：“妈妈，我饿了！”

一天完了，影子俯伏在树底下，我便要在黄昏中回家来。

我将永不同爸爸那样，离开你到城里去作事。

妈妈，如果你不在意，我长大的时候，要做这渡船的船夫。

THE FURTHER BANK

I long to go over there to the further bank of the river,

Where those boats are tied to the bamboo poles in a line;

Where men cross over in their boats in the morning with ploughs on their shoulders to till their far-away fields;

Where the cowherds make their lowing cattle swim across to the riverside pasture;

Whence they all come back home in the evening, leaving the jackals to howl in the island overgrown with weeds.

Mother, if you don't mind, I should like to become the boatman of the ferry when I am grown up.

They say there are strange pools hidden behind that high bank,

Where flocks of wild ducks come when the rains are over, and thick reeds grow round the margins where waterbirds lay their eggs;

Where snipes with their dancing tails stamp their tiny footprints upon the clean soft mud;

Where in the evening the tall grasses crested with white

flowers invite the moonbeam to float upon their waves.

Mother, if you don't mind, I should like to become the boatman of the ferryboat when I am grown up.

I shall cross and cross back from bank to bank, and all the boys and girls of the village will wonder at me while they are bathing.

When the sun climbs the mid sky and morning wears on to noon, I shall come running to you, saying, "Mother, I am hungry!"

When the day is done and the shadows cower under the trees, I shall come back in the dusk.

I shall never go away from you into the town to work like father.

Mother, if you don't mind, I should like to become the boatman of the ferryboat when I am grown up.

花的学校

当雷云在天上轰响，六月的阵雨落下的时候，

润湿的东风走过荒野，在竹林中吹着口笛。

于是一群一群的花从无人知道的地方突然跑出来，在绿草上狂欢的跳着舞。

妈妈，我真的觉得那群花朵是在地下的学校里上学。

他们关了门做功课，如果他们想在散学以前出来游戏，他们的老师是要罚他们站壁角的。

雨一来，他们便放假了。

树枝在林中互相碰触着，绿叶在狂风里萧萧的响着，雷云拍着大手，花孩子们便在那时候穿了紫的、黄的、白的衣裳，冲了出来。

你可知道，妈妈，他们的家是在天上，在星星所住的地方。

你没有看见他们怎样的急着要到那儿去么？你不知道他们为什么那样急急忙忙么？

我自然能够猜得出他们是对谁扬起双臂来：他们也有他们的妈妈，就像我有我自己的妈妈一样。

THE FLOWER-SCHOOL

When storm clouds rumble in the sky and June showers come down,

The moist east wind comes marching over the heath to blow its bagpipes among the bamboos.

Then crowds of flowers come out of a sudden, from nobody knows where, and dance upon the grass in wild glee.

Mother, I really think the flowers go to school underground.

They do their lessons with doors shut, and if they want to come out to play before it is time, their master makes them stand in a corner.

When the rains come they have their holidays.

Branches clash together in the forest, and the leaves rustle in the wild wind, the thunder-clouds clap their giant hands and the flower children rush out in dresses of pink and yellow and white.

Do you know, mother, their home is in the sky, where the

stars are.

Haven't you seen how eager they are to get there? Don't you know why they are in such a hurry?

Of course, I can guess to whom they raise their arms: they have their mother as I have my own.

商 人

妈妈，让我们想像，你待在家里，我到异邦去旅行。

再想像，我的船已经装得满满的在码头上等候启碇了。

现在，妈妈，好生想一想再告诉我，回来的时候我要带些什么给你。

妈妈，你要一堆一堆的黄金么？

在金河的两岸，田野里全是金色的稻实。

在林荫的路上，金色花也一朵一朵的落在地上。

我要为你把它们全都收拾起来，放在好几百个篮子里。

妈妈，你要秋天的雨点一般大的珍珠么？

我要渡海到珍珠岛的岸上去。

那个地方，在清晨的曙光里，珠子在草地的野花上颤动，珠子落在绿草上，珠子被汹狂的海浪一大把一大把的撒在沙滩上。

我的哥哥呢，我要送他一对有翼的马，会在云端飞翔的。

爸爸呢，我要带一支有魔力的笔给他，他还没有觉得，笔就写出字来了。

你呢，妈妈，我一定要把那个值七个国王的王国的首饰箱和珠宝送给你。

THE MERCHANT

Imagine, mother, that you are to stay at home and I am to travel into strange lands.

Imagine that my boat is ready at the landing fully laden.

Now think well, mother, before you say what I shall bring for you when I come back.

Mother, do you want heaps and heaps of gold?

There, by the banks of golden streams, fields are full of golden harvest.

And in the shade of the forest path the golden *champa* flowers drop on the ground.

I will gather them all for you in many hundred baskets.

Mother, do you want pearls big as the raindrops of autumn?

I shall cross to the pearl island shore.

There in the early morning light pearls tremble on the meadow flowers, pearls drop on the grass, and pearls are scattered on the sand in spray by the wild sea-waves.

My brother shall have a pair of horses with wings to fly among the clouds.

For father I shall bring a magic pen that, without his knowing, will write of itself.

For you, mother, I must have the casket and jewel that cost seven kings their kingdoms.

同 情

如果我只是一只小狗，而不是你的小孩，亲爱的妈妈，当我想吃你的盘里的东西时，你要向我说“不”么？

你要赶开我，对我说道，“滚开，你这淘气的小狗”么？

那末，走罢，妈妈，走罢！当你叫唤我的时候，我就永不到你那里去，也永不要你再喂我吃东西了。

如果我只是一只绿色的小鹦鹉，而不是你的小孩，亲爱的妈妈，你要把我紧紧的锁住，怕我飞走么？

你要对我摇你的手，说道，“怎样的一个不知感恩的贱鸟呀！整日整夜的尽在咬它的链子”么？

那末，走罢，妈妈，走罢！我要跑到树林里去；我就永不再让你抱我在你的臂里了。

SYMPATHY

If I were only a little puppy, not your baby, mother dear, would you say "No" to me if I tried to eat from your dish?

Would you drive me off, saying to me, "Get away, you naughty little puppy?"

Then go, mother, go! I will never come to you when you call me, and never let you feed me any more.

If I were only a little green parrot, and not your baby, mother dear, would you keep me chained lest I should fly away?

Would you shake your finger at me and say, "What an ungrateful wretch of a bird! It is gnawing at its chain day and night?"

Then, go, mother, go! I will run away into the woods; I will never let you take me in your arms again.

职 业

早晨，钟敲十下的时候，我沿着我们的小巷到学校去，

每天我都遇见那个小贩，他叫道："镯子呀，亮晶晶的镯子！"

他没有什么事情急着要做，他没有那条街一定要走，他没有什么地方一定要去，他没有什么时间一定要回家。

我愿意我是一个小贩，在街上过日子，叫着："镯子呀，亮晶晶的镯子！"

下午四点，我从学校里回家。

从一家门口，我看得见一个园丁在那里掘地。

他用他的锄子，要怎么掘，便怎么掘，他被尘土污了衣裳，如果他被太阳晒黑了或是身上被打湿了，都没有人骂他。

我愿意我是一个园丁，在花园里掘地，谁也不来阻止我。

天色刚黑，妈妈就送我上床，

从开着的窗口，我看得见更夫走来走去。

小巷又黑又冷清，路灯立在那里，像一个头上生着一只红眼睛的巨人。

更夫摇着他的提灯，跟他身边的影子一起走着，他一生一

次都没有上床去过。

我愿意我是一个更夫，整夜在街上走，提了灯去追逐影子。

VOCATION

When the gong sounds ten in the morning and I walk to school by our lane,

Everyday I meet the hawker crying, "Bangles, crystal bangles!"

There is nothing to hurry him on, there is no road he must take, no place he must go to, no time when he must come home.

I wish I were a hawker, spending my day in the road, crying, "Bangles, crystal bangles!"

When at four in the afternoon I come back from the school,

I can see through the gate of that house the gardener digging the ground.

He does what he likes with his spade, he soils his clothes with dust, nobody takes him to task if he gets baked in the sun or gets wet.

I wish I were a gardener digging away at the garden with nobody to stop me from digging.

Just as it gets dark in the evening and my mother sends me to bed,

I can see through my open window the watchman walking up and down.

The lane is dark and lonely and the street-lamp stands like a giant with one red eye in its head.

The watchman swings his lantern and walks with his shadow at his side, and never once goes to bed in his life.

I wish I were a watchman walking the streets all night, chasing the shadows with my lantern.

长 者

妈妈，你的孩子真傻！她是那末可笑的不懂事！

她不知道路灯和星星的分别。

当我们玩着把小石子当食物的游戏时，她便以为它们真是吃的东西，竟想放进嘴里去。

当我翻开一本书，放在她面前，要她读 a，b，c 时，她却用手把书页撕了，无端快活的叫起来；你的孩子就是这样做功课的。

当我生气的对她摇头，骂她，说她顽皮时，她却哈哈大笑，以为很有趣。

谁都知道爸爸不在家，但是，如果我在游戏时高声叫一声“爸爸”，她便要高兴的四面张望，以为爸爸真是近在身边。

当我把洗衣人带来载衣服回去的驴子当做学生，并且警告她说，我是老师，她却无缘无故的乱叫起我哥哥来。

你的孩子要捉月亮。她是这样的可笑；她把格尼许[①]唤作琪奴许。

妈妈，你的孩子真傻，她是那末可笑的不懂事！

---

① 格尼许，印度常见名字之一，也是印度教中象头神之名。

SUPERIOR

Mother, your baby is silly! She is so absurdly childish!

She does not know the difference between the lights in the streets and the stars.

When we play at eating with pebbles, she thinks they are real food, and tries to put them into her mouth.

When I open a book before her and ask her to learn her a, b, c, she tears the leaves with her hands and roars for joy at nothing; this is your baby's way of doing her lesson.

When I shake my head at her in anger and scold her and call her naughty, she laughs and thinks it great fun.

Everybody knows that father is away, but, if in play I call aloud "Father," she looks about her in excitement and thinks that father is near.

When I hold my class with the donkeys that our washerman brings to carry away the clothes and I warn her that I am the schoolmaster, she will scream for no reason and call me dādā.

Your baby wants to catch the moon. She is so funny; she calls Ganesh Gānush.

Mother, your baby is silly, she is so absurdly childish!

小大人

我人很小，因为我是一个小孩子。到了我像爸爸一样年纪时，便要变大了。

我的先生要是走来说道："时候晚了，把你的石板，你的书拿来。"

我便要告诉他道："你不知道我已经同爸爸一样大了么？我决不再学什么功课了。"

我的老师便将惊异的说道："他读书不读书可以随便，因为他是大人了。"

我将自己穿了衣裳，走到人群拥挤的市场里去。

我的叔叔要是跑过来说道："你要迷路了，我的孩子；让我领着你罢。"

我便要回答道："你没有看见么，叔叔，我已经同爸爸一样大了？我决定要独自一个人到市场里去。"

叔叔便将说道："是的，他随便到那里去都可以，因为他是大人了。"

当我正拿钱给我保姆时，妈妈便要从浴室中出来，因为我是知道怎样用我的钥匙去开银箱的。

妈妈要是说道："你在做什么呀，顽皮的孩子？"

我便要告诉她道："妈妈，你不知道我已经同爸爸一样大了么？我必须拿钱给保姆。"

妈妈便将自言自语道："他可以随便把钱给他所喜欢的人，因为他是大人了。"

当十月里放假的时候，爸爸将要回家，他会以为我还是一个小孩子，为我从城里带了小鞋子和小绸衫来。

我便要说道："爸爸，把这些东西给哥哥罢，因为我已经同你一样大了。"

爸爸便将想了一想，说道："他可以随便去买他自己穿的衣裳，因为他是大人了。"

THE LITTLE BIG MAN

I am small because I am a little child. I shall be big when I am as old as my father is.

My teacher will come and say, "It is late, bring your slate and your books."

I shall tell him, "Do you not know I am as big as father? And I must not have lessons any more."

My master will wonder and say, "He can leave his books if he likes, for he is grown up."

I shall dress myself and walk to the fair where the crowd is thick.

My uncle will come rushing up to me and say, "You will get lost, my boy; let me carry you."

I shall answer, "Can't you see, uncle, I am as big as father? I must go to the fair alone."

Uncle will say, "Yes, he can go wherever he likes, for he is grown up."

Mother will come from her bath when I am giving money to my nurse, for I shall know how to open the box with my key.

Mother will say, "What are you about, naughty child?"

I shall tell her, "Mother, don't you know, I am as big as father, and I must give silver to my nurse."

Mother will say to herself, "He can give money to whom he likes, for he is grown up."

In the holiday time in October father will come home and, thinking that I am still a baby, will bring for me from the town little shoes and small silken frocks.

I shall say, "Father, give them to my dādā, for I am as big as you are."

Father will think and say, "He can buy his own clothes if he likes, for he is grown up."

十二点钟

妈妈，我真想现在不做功课了。我整个早晨都在念书呢。

你说，现在还不过是十二点钟。假定不会晚过十二点罢；难道你不能把不过是十二点钟想像成下午么？

我能够容容易易的想像：现在太阳已经到了那片稻田的边缘上了，老态龙钟的渔婆正在池边采撷香草作她的晚餐。

我闭上了眼就能够想到，马塔尔树[1]下的阴影是更深黑了，池塘里的水看来黑得发亮。

假如十二点钟能够在黑夜里来到，为什么黑夜不能在十二点钟的时候来到呢？

① 马塔尔树，即牛角瓜，是印度传统药用植物。

TWELVE O'CLOCK

Mother, I do want to leave off my lessons now. I have been at my book all the morning.

You say it is only twelve o'clock. Suppose it isn't any later; can't you ever think it is afternoon when it is only twelve o'clock?

I can easily imagine now that the sun has reached the edge of that rice-field, and the old fisher-woman is gathering herbs for her supper by the side of the pond.

I can just shut my eyes and think that the shadows are growing darker under the *madar* tree, and the water in the pond looks shiny black.

If twelve o'clock can come in the night, why can't the night come when it is twelve o'clock?

著作家

你说爸爸写了许多书，但我却不懂得他所写的东西。

他整个黄昏读书给你听，但是你真懂得他的意思么？

妈妈，你给我们讲的故事，真是好听呀！我很奇怪，爸爸为什么不能写那样的书呢？

难道他从来没有从他自己的妈妈那里听见过巨人和神仙和公主的故事么？

还是已经完全忘记了？

他常常耽误了沐浴，你不得不走去叫他一百多次。

你总要等候着，把他的菜温着等他，但他忘了，还尽管写下去。

爸爸老是以著书为游戏。

如果我一走进爸爸房里去游戏，你就要走来叫道："真是一个顽皮的孩子！"

如果我稍为出一点声音，你就要说："你没有看见你爸爸正在工作么？"

老是写了又写，有什么趣味呢？

当我拿起爸爸的钢笔或铅笔，像他一模一样的在他的书上写着，——a，b，c，d，e，f，g，h，i，——那时，你为什么跟我生气呢，妈妈？

爸爸写时，你却从来不说一句话。

当我爸爸耗费了那末一大堆纸时，妈妈，你似乎全不在乎。

但是，如果我只取了一张纸去做一只船，你却要说："孩子，你真讨厌！"

你对于爸爸拿黑点子涂满了纸的两面，污损了许多许多张纸，你心里以为怎样呢？

AUTHORSHIP

You say that father writes a lot of books, but what he writes I don't understand.

He was reading to you all the evening, but could you really make out what he meant?

What nice stories, mother, you can tell us! Why can't father write like that, I wonder?

Did he never hear from his own mother stories of giants and fairies and princesses?

Has he forgotten them all?

Often when he gets late for his bath you have to go and call him an hundred times.

You wait and keep his dishes warm for him, but he goes on writing and forgets.

Father always plays at making books.

If ever I go to play in father's room, you come and call me, "what a naughty child!"

If I make the slightest noise, you say, "Don't you see that

father's at his work?"

What's the fun of always writing and writing?

When I take up father's pen or pencil and write upon his book just as he does, —a, b, c, d, e, f, g, h, i, —why do you get cross with me, then, mother?

You never say a word when father writes.

When my father wastes such heaps of paper, mother, you don't seem to mind at all.

But if I take only one sheet to make a boat with, you say, "Child, how troublesome you are!"

What do you think of father's spoiling sheets and sheets of paper with black marks all over on both sides?

恶邮差

你为什么坐在那边地板上不言不动的，告诉我呀，亲爱的妈妈？

雨从开着的窗口打进来了，把你身上全打湿了，你却不管。

你听见钟已打四下了么？正是哥哥从学校里回家的时候了。

到底发生了什么事，你的神色这样不对？

你今天没有接到爸爸的信么？

我看见邮差在他的袋里带了许多信来，几乎镇里的每个人都分送到了。

只有爸爸的信，他留起来给他自己看。我确信这个邮差是个坏人。

但是不要因此不乐呀，亲爱的妈妈。

明天是邻村市集的日子。你叫女仆去买些笔和纸来。

我自己会写爸爸所写的一切信；使你找不出一点错处来。

我要从 A 字一直写到 K 字。

但是，妈妈，你为什么笑呢？

你不相信我能写得同爸爸一样好！

但是我将用心画格子，把所有的字母都写得又大又美。

当我写好了时，你以为我也像爸爸那样傻，把它投入可怕的邮差的袋中么？

我立刻就自己送来给你，而且一个字母、一个字母的帮助你读。

我知道那邮差是不肯把真正的好信送给你的。

THE WICKED POSTMAN

Why do you sit there on the floor so quiet and silent, tell me, mother dear?

The rain is coming in through the open window, making you all wet, and you don't mind it.

Do you hear the gong striking four? It is time for my brother to come home from school.

What has happened to you that you look so strange?

Haven't you got a letter from father to-day?

I saw the postman bringing letters in his bag for almost everybody in the town.

Only, father's letters he keeps to read himself. I am sure the postman is a wicked man.

But don't be unhappy about that, mother dear.

To-morrow is market day in the next village. You ask your maid to buy some pens and papers.

I myself will write all father's letters; you will not find a single mistake.

I shall write from A right up to K.

But, mother, why do you smile?

You don't believe that I can write as nicely as father does!

But I shall rule my paper carefully, and write all the letters beautifully big.

When I finish my writing, do you think I shall be so foolish as father and drop it into the horrid postman's bag?

I shall bring it to you myself without waiting, and letter by letter help you to read my writing.

I know the postman does not like to give you the really nice letters.

英 雄

妈妈，让我们想像我们正在旅行，经过一个陌生而危险的国土。

你坐在一顶轿子里，我骑着一匹红马，在你旁边跑着。

是黄昏的时候，太阳已经下山了。约拉地希的荒地疲乏而灰暗的展开在我们面前。大地是凄凉而荒芜的。

你害怕了，想道——“我不知道我们到了什么地方了。”

我对你说道：“妈妈，不要害怕。”

草地上刺蓬蓬的长着针尖似的草，一条狭而崎岖的小道通过这块草地。

在这片广大的地面上看不见一只牛；它们已经回到它们村里的牛棚去了。

天色黑了下来，大地和天空都显得朦朦胧胧的，而我们不能说出我们正走向什么所在。

突然间，你叫我，悄悄的问我道：“靠近河岸的是什么火光呀？”

正在那个时候，一阵可怕的呐喊声爆发了，好些人影子向我们跑过来。

你蹲坐在你的轿子里，嘴里反覆的祷念着神的名字。

轿夫们，怕得发抖，躲藏在荆棘丛中。

我向你喊道："不要害怕，妈妈，有我在这里。"

他们手里执着长棒，头发披散着，越走越近了。

我喊道："要当心！你们这些坏蛋！再向前走一步，你们就要送命了。"

他们又发出一阵可怕的呐喊声，向前冲过来。

你抓住我的手，说道："好孩子，看在上天面上，躲开他们罢。"

我说道："妈妈，你瞧我的。"

于是我刺策着我的马匹，猛奔过去，我的剑和盾彼此碰着作响。

这一场战斗是那末激烈，妈妈，如果你从轿子里看得见的话，你一定会发冷战的。

他们之中，许多人逃走了，还有好些人被砍杀了。

我知道你那时独自坐在那里，心里正在想着，你的孩子这时候一定已经死了。

但是我跑到你的跟前，浑身溅满了鲜血，说道："妈妈，现在战争已经结束了。"

你从轿子里走出来，吻着我，把我搂在你的心头，你自言自语的说道：

"如果我没有我的孩子护送我，我简直不知道怎么办才好。"

一千件无聊的事天天在发生，为什么这样一件事不能够偶然实现呢?

这很像一本书里的一个故事。

我的哥哥要说道：“这是可能的事么？我老是想，他是那末嫩弱呢！”

我们村里的人们都要惊讶的说道：“这孩子正和他妈妈在一起，这不是很幸运么？”

THE HERO

Mother, let us imagine we are travelling, and passing through a strange and dangerous country.

You are riding in a palanquin and I am trotting by you on a red horse.

It is evening and the sun goes down. The waste of *Joradighi* lies wan and grey before us. The land is desolate and barren.

You are frightened and thinking—"I know not where we have come to."

I say to you, "Mother, do not be afraid."

The meadow is prickly with spiky grass, and through it runs a narrow broken path.

There are no cattle to be seen in the wide field; they have gone to their village stalls.

It grows dark and dim on the land and sky, and we cannot tell where we are going.

Suddenly you call me and ask me in a whisper, "What light is that near the bank?"

Just then there bursts out a fearful yell, and figures come running towards us.

You sit crouched in your palanquin and repeat the names of the gods in prayer.

The bearers, shaking in terror, hide themselves in the thorny bush.

I shout to you, "Don't be afraid, mother. I am here."

With long sticks in their hands and hair all wild about their heads, they come nearer and nearer.

I shout, "Have a care! you villains! One step more and you are dead men."

They give another terrible yell and rush forward.

You clutch my hand and say, "Dear boy, for heaven's sake, keep away from them."

I say, "Mother, just you watch me."

Then I spur my horse for a wild gallop, and my sword and buckler clash against each other.

The fight becomes so fearful, mother, that it would give you a cold shudder could you see it from your palanquin.

Many of them fly, and a great number are cut to pieces.

I know you are thinking, sitting all by yourself, that your boy must be dead by this time.

But I come to you all stained with blood, and say, "Mother, the fight is over now."

You come out and kiss me, pressing me to your heart, and you say to yourself,

"I don't know what I should do if I hadn't my boy to escort me."

A thousand useless things happen day after day, and why couldn't such a thing come true by chance?

It would be like a story in a book.

My brother would say, "Is it possible? I always thought he was so delicate!"

Our village people would all say in amazement, "Was it not lucky that the boy was with his mother?"

告 别

是我走的时候了，妈妈；我走了。

当清寂的黎明，你在暗中伸出双臂，要抱你睡在床上的孩子时，我要说道："孩子不在那里呀！"——妈妈，我走了。

我要变成一股清风抚摸着你；我要变成水中的涟漪，当你浴时，把你吻了又吻。

大风之夜，当雨点在树叶中淅沥时，你在床上，会听见我的微语，当电光从开着的窗口闪进你的屋里时，我的笑声也偕了它一同闪进了。

如果你醒着躺在床上，想你的孩子到深夜，我便要从星空向你唱道："睡呀！妈妈，睡呀。"

我要坐在各处游荡的月光上，偷偷的来到你的床上，乘你睡着时，躺在你的胸上。

我要变成一个梦儿，从你的眼皮的微缝中，钻到你的睡眠的深处，当你醒来吃惊的四望时，我便如闪耀的萤火似的熠熠的向暗中飞去了。

当普耶[①]大祭日，邻家的孩子们来屋里游玩时，我便要融化

① 普耶，来自梵语，意为"崇拜"，是印度教中一种祭拜典礼或一个宗教节日。

在笛声里，整日价在你心头震荡。

亲爱的阿姨带了普耶礼[①]来，问道："我们的孩子在那里，姊姊？"妈妈，你将要柔声的告诉她："他呀，他现在是在我的瞳人里，他现在是在我的身体里，在我的灵魂里。"

① 普耶礼，指某个普耶节日里人们相互赠送的礼物。

THE END

It is time for me to go, mother; I am going.

When in the paling darkness of the lonely dawn you stretch out your arms for your baby in the bed, I shall say, "Baby is not there!"—mother, I am going.

I shall become a delicate draught of air and caress you; and I shall be ripples in the water when you bathe, and kiss you and kiss you again.

In the gusty night when the rain patters on the leaves you will hear my whisper in your bed, and my laughter will flash with the lightning through the open window into your room.

If you lie awake, thinking of your baby till late into the night, I shall sing to you from the stars, "Sleep, mother, sleep."

On the straying moonbeams I shall steal over your bed, and lie upon your bosom while you sleep.

I shall become a dream, and through the little opening of your eyelids I shall slip into the depths of your sleep; and when you wake up and look round startled, like a twinkling firefly I shall flit out into the darkness.

When, on the great festival of *puja*, the neighbours' children come and play about the house, I shall melt into the music of the flute and throb in your heart all day.

Dear auntie will come with *puja*-presents and will ask, "Where is our baby, sister?" Mother, you will tell her softly, "He is in the pupils of my eyes, he is in my body and in my soul."

召　唤

她走的时候，夜间黑漆漆的，他们都睡了。

现在，夜间也是黑漆漆的，我唤她道："回来，我的宝贝；世界都在沉睡；当星星互相凝视的时候，你来一会儿是没有人会知道的。"

她走的时候，树木正在萌芽，春光刚刚来到。

现在花已盛开，我唤道："回来，我的宝贝。孩子们漫不经心的在游戏，把花聚在一块，又把它们散开。你如走来，拿一朵小花去，没有人会发觉的。"

常常在游戏的那些人，仍然还在那里游戏，生命总是如此的浪费。

我静听他们的空谈，便唤道："回来，我的宝贝，妈妈的心里充满着爱，你如走来，仅仅从她那里接一个小小的吻，没有人会妒忌的。"

THE RECALL

The night was dark when she went away, and they slept.

The night is dark now, and I call for her, "Come back, my darling; the world is asleep; and no one would know, if you came for a moment while stars are gazing at stars."

She went away when the trees were in bud and the spring was young.

Now the flowers are in high bloom and I call, "Come back, my darling. The children gather and scatter flowers in reckless sport. And if you come and take one little blossom no one will miss it."

Those that used to play are playing still, so spendthrift is life.

I listen to their chatter and call, "Come back, my darling, for mother's heart is full to the brim with love, and if you come to snatch only one little kiss from her no one will grudge it."

第一次的茉莉

呵，这些茉莉花，这些白的茉莉花！

我仿佛记得我第一次双手满捧着这些茉莉花，这些白的茉莉花的时候。

我喜爱那日光，那天空，那绿色的大地；

我听见那河水淙淙的流声，在黑漆的午夜里传过来；

秋天的夕阳，在荒原上大路转角处迎我，如新妇揭起她的面纱迎接她的爱人。

但我想起孩提时第一次捧在手里的白茉莉，心里充满着甜蜜的回忆。

我生平有过许多快活的日子，在节日宴会的晚上，我曾跟着说笑话的人大笑。

在灰暗的雨天的早晨，我吟哦过许多飘逸的诗篇。

我颈上戴过爱人手织的醉花的花圈，作为晚装。

但我想起孩提时第一次捧在手里的白茉莉，心里充满着甜蜜的回忆。

THE FIRST JASMINES

Ah, these jasmines, these white jasmines!

I seem to remember the first day when I filled my hands with these jasmines, these white jasmines.

I have loved the sunlight, the sky and the green earth;

I have heard the liquid murmur of the river through the darkness of midnight;

Autumn sunsets have come to me at the bend of a road in the lonely waste, like a bride raising her veil to accept her lover.

Yet my memory is still sweet with the first white jasmines that I held in my hand when I was a child.

Many a glad day has come in my life, and I have laughed with merrymakers on festival nights.

On grey mornings of rain I have crooned many an idle song.

I have worn round my neck the evening wreath of *bakulas* woven by the hand of love.

Yet my heart is sweet with the memory of the first fresh jasmines that filled my hands when I was a child.

榕 树

喂，你站在池边的蓬头的榕树，你可曾忘记了那小小的孩子，就像那在你的枝上筑巢又离开了你的鸟儿似的孩子？

你不记得他怎样坐在窗内，诧异的望着你深入地下的纠缠的树根么？

妇人们常到池边，汲了满罐的水去，你的大黑影便在水面上摇动，好像睡着的人挣扎着要醒来似的。

日光在微波上跳舞，好像不停不息的小梭在织着金色的花毡。

两只鸭子挨着芦苇，在芦苇影子上游来游去，孩子静静的坐在那里想着。

他想做风，吹过你的萧萧的枝杈；想做你的影子，在水面上，随了日光而俱长；想做一只鸟儿，栖息在你的最高枝上；还想做那两只鸭，在芦苇与阴影中间游来游去。

THE BANYAN TREE

O you shaggy-headed banyan tree standing on the bank of the pond, have you forgotten the little child, like the birds that have nested in your branches and left you?

Do you not remember how he sat at the window and wondered at the tangle of your roots that plunged underground?

The women would come to fill their jars in the pond, and your huge black shadow would wriggle on the water like sleep struggling to wake up.

Sunlight danced on the ripples like restless tiny shuttles weaving golden tapestry.

Two ducks swam by the weedy margin above their shadows, and the child would sit still and think.

He longed to be the wind and blow through your rustling branches, to be your shadow and lengthen with the day on the water, to be a bird and perch on your topmost twig, and to float like those ducks among the weeds and shadows.

祝 福

祝福这个小心灵，这个洁白的灵魂，他为我们的大地，赢得了天的接吻。

他爱日光，他爱见他妈妈的脸。

他没有学会厌恶尘土而渴求黄金。

紧抱他在你心里，并且祝福他。

他已来到这个歧路百出的大地上了。

我不知道他怎么从群众中选出你来，来到你的门前抓住你的手问路。

他笑着，谈着，跟着你走，心里没有一点儿疑惑。

不要辜负他的信任，引导他到正路，并且祝福他。

把你的手按在他的头上，祈求着：底下的波涛虽然险恶，然而从上面来的风，会鼓起他的船帆，送他到和平的港口的。

不要在忙碌中把他忘了，让他来到你的心里，并且祝福他。

BENEDICTION

Bless this little heart, this white soul that has won the kiss of heaven for our earth.

He loves the light of the sun, he loves the sight of his mother's face.

He has not learned to despise the dust, and to hanker after gold.

Clasp him to your heart and bless him.

He has come into this land of an hundred cross-roads.

I know not how he chose you from the crowd, came to your door, and grasped your hand to ask his way.

He will follow you, laughing and talking, and not a doubt in his heart.

Keep his trust, lead him straight and bless him.

Lay your hand on his head, and pray that though the waves underneath grow threatening, yet the breath from above may come and fill his sails and waft him to the haven of peace.

Forget him not in your hurry, let him come to your heart and bless him.

赠 品

我要送些东西给你，我的孩子，因为我们同是漂泊在世界的溪流中的。

我们的生命将被分开，我们的爱也将被忘记。

但我却没有那样傻，希望能用我的赠品来买你的心。

你的生命正是青青，你的道路也长着呢，你一口气饮尽了我们带给你的爱，便回身离开我们跑了。

你有你的游戏，有你的游伴。如果你没有时间同我们在一起，如果你想不到我们，那有什么害处呢？

我们呢，自然的，在老年时，会有许多闲暇的时间，去计算那过去的日子，把我们手里永久失了的东西，在心里爱抚着。

河流唱着歌很快的流去，冲破所有的堤防。但是山峰却留在那里，忆念着，满怀依依之情。

THE GIFT

I want to give you something, my child, for we are drifting in the stream of the world.

Our lives will be carried apart, and our love forgotten.

But I am not so foolish as to hope that I could buy your heart with my gifts.

Young is your life, your path long, and you drink the love we bring you at one draught and turn and run away from us.

You have your play and your playmates. What harm is there if you have no time or thought for us?

We, indeed, have leisure enough in old age to count the days that are past, to cherish in our hearts what our hands have lost for ever.

The river runs swift with a song, breaking through all barriers. But the mountain stays and remembers, and follows her with his love.

我的歌

我的孩子，我这一只歌将扬起它的乐声围绕你的身旁，好像那爱情的热恋的手臂一样。

我这一只歌将触着你的前额，好像那祝福的接吻一样。

当你只是一个人的时候，它将坐在你的身旁，在你耳边微语着；当你在人群中的时候，它将围住你，使你超然物外。

我的歌将成为你的梦的翼膀，它将把你的心移送到不可知的岸边。

当黑夜覆盖在你路上的时候，它又将成为那照临在你头上的忠实的星光。

我的歌又将坐在你眼睛的瞳人里，将你的视线带入万物的心里。

当我的声音因死亡而沉寂时，我的歌仍将在你活泼泼的心中唱着。

MY SONG

This song of mine will wind its music around you, my child, like the fond arms of love.

This song of mine will touch your forehead like a kiss of blessing.

When you are alone it will sit by your side and whisper in your ear, when you are in the crowd it will fence you about with aloofness.

My song will be like a pair of wings to your dreams, it will transport your heart to the verge of the unknown.

It will be like the faithful star overhead when dark night is over your road.

My song will sit in the pupils of your eyes, and will carry your sight into the heart of things.

And when my voice is silent in death, my song will speak in your living heart.

孩子天使

他们喧哗争斗，他们怀疑失望，他们辩论而没有结果。

我的孩子，让你的生命到他们当中去，如一线镇定而纯洁之光，使他们愉悦而沉默。

他们的贪心和妒忌是残忍的；他们的话，好像暗藏的刀，渴欲饮血。

我的孩子，去，去站在他们愤懑的心中，把你的和善的眼光落在它们上面，好像那傍晚的宽洪大量的和平，覆盖着日间的骚扰一样。

我的孩子，让他们望着你的脸，因此能够知道一切事物的意义；让他们爱你，因此他们能够相爱。

来，坐在无垠的胸膛上，我的孩子。朝阳出来时，开放而且抬起你的心，像一朵盛开的花；夕阳落下时，低下你的头，默默的做完这一天的礼拜。

THE CHILD-ANGEL

They clamour and fight, they doubt and despair, they know no end to their wranglings.

Let your life come amongst them like a flame of light, my child, unflickering and pure, and delight them into silence.

They are cruel in their greed and their envy, their words are like hidden knives thirsting for blood.

Go and stand amidst their scowling hearts, my child, and let your gentle eyes fall upon them like the forgiving peace of the evening over the strife of the day.

Let them see your face, my child, and thus know the meaning of all things; let them love you and thus love each other.

Come and take your seat in the bosom of the limitless, my child. At sunrise open and raise your heart like a blossoming flower, and at sunset bend your head and in silence complete the worship of the day.

最后的买卖

早晨，我在石铺的路上走时，我叫道："谁来雇用我呀。"
皇帝坐着马车，手里拿着剑走来。
他拉着我的手，说道："我要用权力来雇用你。"
但是他的权力算不了什么，他坐着马车走了。

正午炎热的时候，家家户户的门都闭着。
我沿着屈曲的小巷走去。
一个老人带着一袋金钱走出来。
他斟酌了一下，说道："我要用金钱来雇用你。"
他一个一个的数着他的钱，但我却转身离去了。

黄昏了。花园的篱上满开着花。
美人走出来，说道："我要用微笑来雇用你。"
她的微笑黯淡了，化成泪容了，她孤寂的回身走进黑暗里去。

太阳照耀在沙地上，海波任性的浪花四溅。
一个小孩坐在那里玩贝壳。
他抬起头来，好像认识我似的，说道："我雇你不用什么么东西。”

从此以后，在这个小孩的游戏中做成的买卖，使我成了一个自由的人。

THE LAST BARGAIN

"Come and hire me," I cried, while in the morning I was walking on the stone-paved road.

Sword in hand, the King came in his chariot.

He held my hand and said, "I will hire you with my power."

But his power counted for nought, and he went away in his chariot.

In the heat of the midday the houses stood with shut doors.

I wandered along the crooked lane.

An old man came out with his bag of gold.

He pondered and said, "I will hire you with my money."

He weighed his coins one by one, but I turned away.

It was evening. The garden hedge was all aflower.

The fair maid came out and said, "I will hire you with a smile."

Her smile paled and melted into tears, and she went back alone into the dark.

The sun glistened on the sand, and the sea waves broke waywardly.

A child sat playing with shells.

He raised his head and seemed to know me, and said, "I hire you with nothing."

From thenceforward that bargain struck in child's play made me a free man.